COBBLESTONE · THE CIVIL WAR

Nation at War

Soldiers, Saints, and Spies

Cobblestone Publishing
A Division of Carus Publishing
Peterborough, NH
www.cobblestonepub.com

Staff

Editorial Director: Lou Waryncia

Editor: Sarah Elder Hale

Book Design: David Nelson, www.dnelsondesign.com

Proofreaders: Meg Chorlian, Eileen Terrill

Text Credits

The content of this volume is derived from articles that first appeared in *COBBLESTONE* and *APPLESEEDS* magazines. Contributors: Cynthia Butler, Cornelia Erskine, Robert Feeman, Meg Galante-DeAngelis, Sarah Elder Hale, Lloyd Linford, Walter Oleksy, William Robertson, Jean-Rae Turner, Nancy Whitelaw

Picture Credits

Photos.com: 3, 8 (bottom), 14, 24, 29, 30; Library of Congress: 4–5, 13, 17, 23, 26, 27, 32; Clipart.com: 6, 7, 8 (top), 9, 18–19, 20, 21, 25, 28, 35, 41, 42, 43; Fred Carlson: 10–11, 44–45; Reynolds Historical Library, the University of Alabama at Birmingham: 16; Wisconsin Historical Society: 36–37, 37, 38, 40. Images for "Civil War Time Line," pages 44–45, courtesy of Photos.com, Clipart.com, and Library of Congress.

Cover

Fight for the Standard

Reproduced courtesy of the Wadsworth Atheneum Museum of Art, Hartford, CT. The Ella Gallup Sumner and Mary Catlin Sumner Collection Fund.

Library of Congress Cataloging-in-Publication Data

Nation at war : soldiers, saints, and spies / [project director, Lou Waryncia; editor, Sarah Elder Hale].

    p. cm. -- (Cobblestone the Civil War)

    Includes index.

    ISBN 0-8126-7900-8 (hardcover)

    1. United States--History--Civil War, 1861-1865--Juvenile literature. 2. United States--History--Civil War, 1861-1865--Social aspects—Juvenile literature. 3. United States--History—Civil War, 1861-1865--Biography –Juvenile literature.

    I. Hale, Sarah Elder. II. Waryncia, Lou. III. Series.

E468.N37 2005

973.7--dc22   2005015212

Printed in China

Cobblestone Publishing, Inc.

30 Grove Street, Suite C

Peterborough, NH 03458

www.cobblestonepub.com

Table of Contents

The Dis-United States of America

On March 4, 1861, President-elect Abraham Lincoln was worried as he prepared to take office as the 16th president of the United States. He had just completed a 2,000-mile trip from his home in Illinois, visiting five Northern states and making more than 20 speeches in an attempt to calm the people who had elected him.

Torn in Two

At the time of Lincoln's inauguration, seven Southern states had already seceded from the Union. They refused to accept Lincoln as their president. They elected their own Jefferson Davis as the first president of the newly formed nation called the Confederate States of America. And now, as Lincoln prepared to take office, four more slaveholding states were ready to join their seven Southern neighbors.

Two presidents; two constitutions; two nations, each insisting on its own sovereignty. Was it lawful for states to withdraw from the Union and form their own confederation? Was the Constitution of the United States only a compact that states might, or might not, agree to uphold? Could certain states, through legal proceedings, bring their participation in the Union to an end?

In four years, 384 battles (and many more small armed conflicts) were fought in the "War Between the States." This print depicts the Battle of Opequon (Virginia).

4

For years these questions had been debated, but without resolution. The North and the South had grown apart, developing different ways of life with different kinds of problems. To the South, compromise no longer seemed possible. It wanted to govern itself as a separate nation. To the North, the formation of the Confederate States of America was widely thought to be treason. Confrontation between the North and the South seemed unavoidable. And on April 12, 1861, when the Confederates attacked Fort Sumter at Charleston, South Carolina, the war finally began.

The War Between the States

The Confederates called the confrontation the "War Between the States." The federal War Department under Lincoln called it the

Key Players

Abraham Lincoln
(1809–1865)

As president of the United States, Abraham Lincoln also served as commander in chief of the Union army. One of his most important duties as the highest-ranking military officer in the land was to appoint able generals to command his troops. Lincoln was assassinated at Ford's Theatre in Washington, D.C., by John Wilkes Booth on April 14, 1865 — just five days after the Confederacy had surrendered to end the Civil War.

Jefferson Davis

(1808–1889)

Jefferson Davis was the president of the Confederate States of America and the commander in chief of the Confederate army. Davis was well qualified for both jobs. He had served as a colonel in the U.S. Army during the U.S.–Mexican War, had been secretary of war in President Franklin Pierce's cabinet, and had served as a member of the U.S. Senate. After the Civil War, Davis served two years in prison for treason against the United States.

"War of the Rebellion." Those who tried to understand the war from a constitutional point of view called it the "War of Secession." But no matter what they called it, few people believed that it would last very long — maybe three months at the longest. The North hoped that the South was not serious about its new confederacy, and the South hoped that the North would soon give in and let it go its separate way.

But each side underestimated the other. And it wasn't long before both sides realized that there was nothing more brutal and tragic than the hand-to-hand combat of a civil war.

North vs. South

In 1861, when the war began, there were approximately 18 million people living in the North, and the North controlled practically two-thirds of the nation's railroads. The North had nine-tenths of the nation's industry and most of the raw materials needed to keep its factories going.

The South had only half as many people as the North, and one-third of its population were slaves. With fewer troops, fewer guns and ammunition, and fewer supplies to keep the soldiers clothed and fed, the South appeared to be at a tremendous disadvantage.

The South, however, had one important advantage over the North that probably kept the war going for as long as it did. The South fought almost the entire war, with the exception of two battles, on its own soil. The North was forced to invade the South, shipping supplies across enemy lines and camping in unfamiliar, unfriendly territory.

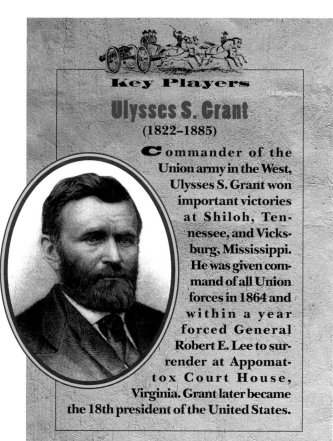

Key Players

Ulysses S. Grant
(1822–1885)

Commander of the Union army in the West, Ulysses S. Grant won important victories at Shiloh, Tennessee, and Vicksburg, Mississippi. He was given command of all Union forces in 1864 and within a year forced General Robert E. Lee to surrender at Appomattox Court House, Virginia. Grant later became the 18th president of the United States.

General Grant and General Lee

When General Ulysses S. Grant took command of the Union army, he planned to keep attacking the South until the Confederates were worn down, no matter how many lives were lost. In order to trap the Confederate army, he turned his western army over to General William Tecumseh Sherman, with orders to move in behind Confederate general Robert E. Lee. Sherman began his march across Georgia, destroying Confederate supplies that lay in his path.

In the meantime, Grant's own army

A Musical War

Musicians had several roles to play in the army. Regiments and brigades often included brass bands. Drums were a way to mark time and signal orders. Cavalry units used bugles to communicate commands.

began a battle with Lee's that became one of the worst in American military history. All through the summer of 1864, Grant tried to get his army across the Rappahannock River in northern Virginia, while Lee resisted his attempts. At Cold Harbor, just 10 miles from Richmond, Virginia, Grant lost 12,000 men in half an hour. In fact, Grant lost more men than Lee had in his entire army, but he was able to replace his losses with fresh troops. Lee also suffered heavy losses. His army was reduced to half of its original size, but for him, there were no replacements.

Early in April 1865, Lee abandoned Petersburg and Richmond to the Union army. He tried to move his army west, but his movements were blocked. On April 9, surrounded by Union troops, Lee surrendered to Grant at Appomattox Court House. Sherman forced the remaining Confederate resistance to surrender near Durham, North Carolina, and the war was over.

War's Aftermath

Now began the work of rebuilding a tattered nation still divided by different ways of life and very different needs. This period is called Reconstruction (1865–1877). The question of whether it was lawful for a state to secede from the Union had been resolved by war. The practice of slavery in America had been abolished. During Reconstruction, the people of the reunited nation had difficult challenges to face: addressing the economic needs of the South, bringing together the government, and integrating the newly freed slaves into society. The war was over, but many battles lay ahead for the people and leaders of the United States.

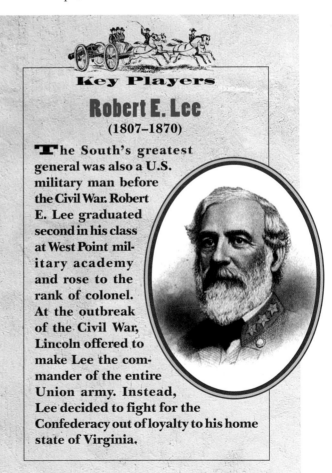

Key Players

Robert E. Lee
(1807–1870)

The South's greatest general was also a U.S. military man before the Civil War. Robert E. Lee graduated second in his class at West Point military academy and rose to the rank of colonel. At the outbreak of the Civil War, Lincoln offered to make Lee the commander of the entire Union army. Instead, Lee decided to fight for the Confederacy out of loyalty to his home state of Virginia.

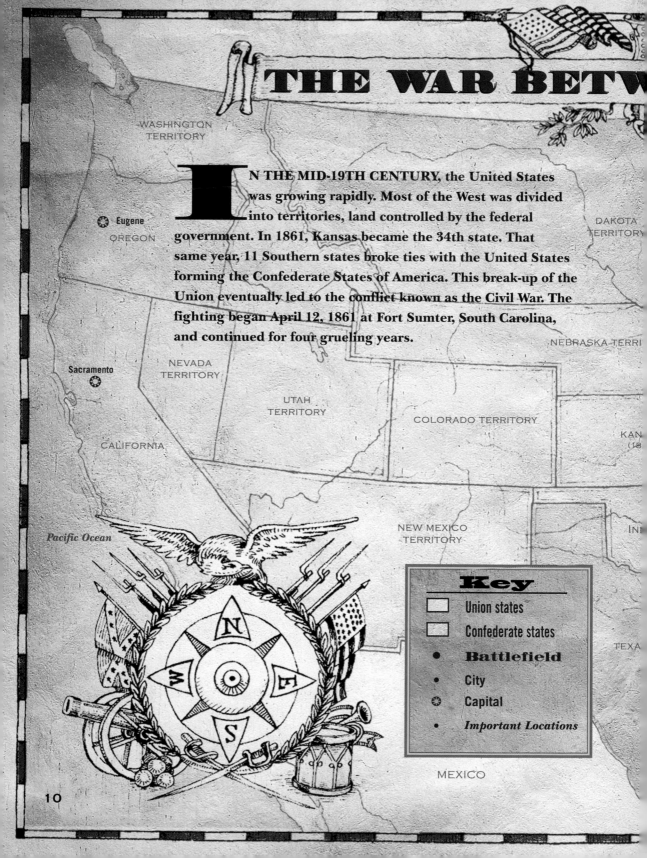

THE WAR BETW

WASHINGTON
TERRITORY

Eugene
OREGON

DAKOTA
TERRITORY

IN THE MID-19TH CENTURY, the United States was growing rapidly. Most of the West was divided into territories, land controlled by the federal government. In 1861, Kansas became the 34th state. That same year, 11 Southern states broke ties with the United States forming the Confederate States of America. This break-up of the Union eventually led to the conflict known as the Civil War. The fighting began April 12, 1861 at Fort Sumter, South Carolina, and continued for four grueling years.

NEBRASKA TERRI

Sacramento

NEVADA
TERRITORY

UTAH
TERRITORY

COLORADO TERRITORY

KAN
(18

CALIFORNIA

Pacific Ocean

NEW MEXICO
TERRITORY

IN

Key

☐ Union states

☐ Confederate states

● **Battlefield**

• City

◉ Capital

• *Important Locations*

TEXA

MEXICO

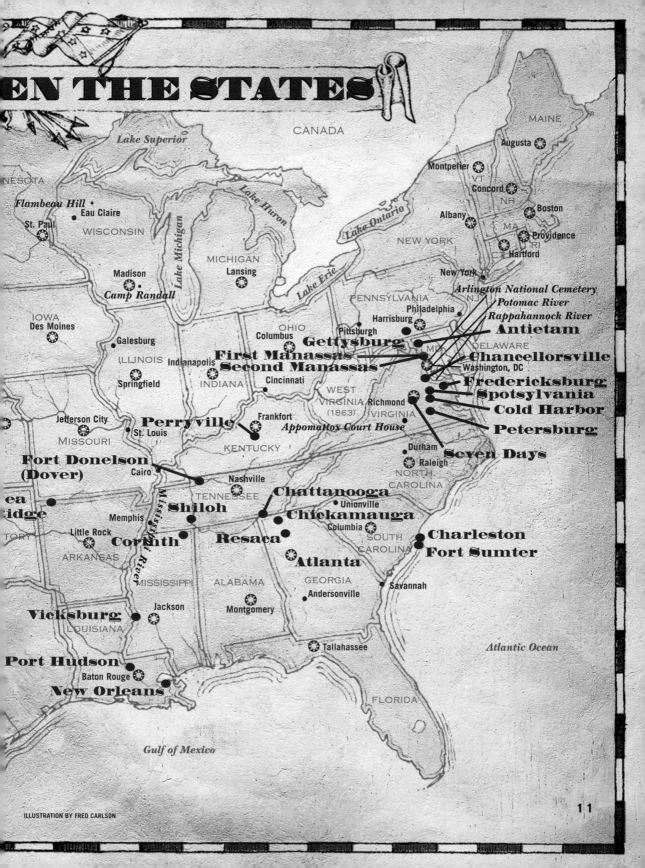

Cyclone in Calico

In 1888, a group of Civil War veterans were at a meeting in Topeka, Kansas. Suddenly, near the door, a great cheer went up.

"Mother Bickerdyke is here!" was the excited reply. "The meeting can wait!"

"I knew her at once," said one veteran, "though her hair has turned to white."

"I knew her by the tender eyes and the kind mouth," said another. "I shall never forget how good they looked to me after the battle of Resaca, where I lost my foot, and gave myself up to die, I was in such pain. I tell you, it seemed as if my own mother was doing for me, she was so gentle." And he wiped his wet eyes with the back of his hand.

The men pressed forward to greet her. Many of them remembered her personally, for Mary Ann Bickerdyke had tended thousands of sick and wounded during the Civil War.

Makeshift Hospitals

When the war began, the Union army was totally unprepared to care for casualties. Makeshift hospitals soon sprang up, but they were dirty and poorly supplied and lacked proper nurses. Soldiers sometimes wrote letters about the hospital conditions. The following letter was sent from Camp Griffen, near Washington, D.C., on November 12, 1861.

I suppose you would like to hear what we are doing in Virginia in the way of bringing the rebels to subjection. As yet we have done little fighting, but have lost a large number of men. They are dying daily in the camps and hospitals from pneumonia, dysentery, and camp diseases, caused by severe colds, exposure, and lack of proper food when ill.

We have taken very heavy colds lying on our arms in line of battle, long frosty nights. For two days and nights there was a very severe storm, to which we were exposed all the time, wearing shoddy uniforms and protected only by shoddy blankets, and the result was a frightful amount of sickness. We have about thirty in our regimental hospital who will never again be good for anything, if they live.

Fast Fact

Of the 624,000 deaths during the Civil War, about **1 out of 3** were the result of sickness.

Our hospitals are so bad that the men fight against being sent to them. They will not go until they are compelled, and many brave it out and die in camp. I really believe they are more comfortable and better cared for in camp, with their comrades, than in the hospital.

In the hospital the nurses are "convalescent soldiers," so nearly sick themselves that they ought to be in the wards, and from their very feebleness they are selfish and sometimes inhuman in their treatment of the patients.

We need beds and bedding, hospital clothing and sick-diet, proper medicines, surgical instruments, and good nurses, and then a decent building or a good hospital tent for the accommodation of our sick. I suppose we shall have them when the government can get around to it, and in the meantime we try to be patient.

Taking Action

Mother Bickerdyke was not patient! When war broke out, she was a 44-year-old widow living in Galesburg, Illinois. Boys from her own town were dying, just like those in the letter. They had not yet left

Wounded soldiers get some fresh air at a military hospital in Fredericksburg, Virginia. Inset: Mary Ann "Mother" Bickerdyke was a harsh critic of hospital conditions, but she was all heart when it came to the soldiers she tended.

Peaches

The hospital kitchen Mother Bickerdyke set up had barely enough basic food, such as beef broth, tea, and bread. Special items were rare indeed. One time some folks from Illinois sent a case of dried peaches. She warned the cook one more time, "These are for sick men, not well ones. Keep your hands off 'em!"

She stewed up the lot, with plenty of brown sugar and cinnamon, and left them to cool: "Just you remember, now. Not a soul touches these peaches. They's for my sick boys."

As she watched from another room, the usual parade of staff members invaded the kitchen. Strange sounds began to seep through its closed door. She flung it open so as to let her patients enjoy the sight. All over the kitchen floor, retching men cursed and groaned in pain, clutching their stomachs.

Mother Bickerdyke was not ready with sympathy this time. "What's the matter, fellows?" she asked cheerfully. "Peaches don't agree with you, huh? Well, let me tell you, you're lucky. All you got was a little emetic to make you vomit. Next time it'll be rat poison, and then you will have something to groan about. When I tell you to leave the patients' food alone, I mean it!"

Illinois, much less seen battle. It was more than she could bear.

With money raised by the town, she went to their aid in Cairo, Illinois, with food, clothing, and disinfectant. She took the supplies and stayed, against all rules. The army could not do without her. One way or another, she kept her patients clean, warm, and fed. If that meant breaking rules or taking shortcuts, it was nothing to her. It was with good reason that she was called a "cyclone in calico." As she told one meddling doctor, "I guess you hadn't better get into a row with me, for whenever anybody does, one of us two always goes to the wall, and 'tain't never me!"

Bickerdyke's work in Cairo established her reputation. She was loved by the patients, trusted by the generals, feared and respected by those in between. A certain surgeon, given to drunkenness, ordered her out of his hospital. She replied, "I shall stay as long as the people need me. If you put me out of one door, I shall come in at another. If you bar all the doors against me, I shall come in at the windows, and the patients will help me in! When anyone leaves, it will be you, not me!"

General Ulysses S. Grant saw the good results of Mother Bickerdyke's straightforward, no-nonsense methods. He took her side in disputes and left her alone to do her work, as did General Benjamin M. Prentiss.

'Mother! Mother!'

Some system and order began to be seen at the Cairo hospitals. Battles were fought, and the sick were joined by the wounded. After the battle of Fort Donelson, Bickerdyke helped in the transportation of injured soldiers. Cries of "Mother! Mother!" were heard as she went among them. When all the wounded had at last been removed from the field, rescue parties returned to Cairo for badly needed rest. Darkness fell. Looking from his tent at midnight, an officer saw a faint light flitting back and forth on the abandoned battlefield. It was Mother Bickerdyke, with a lantern, searching among the dead lest some poor soul lay there, still alive.

From the hospitals established at Cairo, Bickerdyke moved on to field hospitals hurriedly set up near battle lines. After Shiloh, Tennessee, she was in a dozen places at once, tending kettles of soup for the wounded and dressing their wounds as well. A surgeon, newly arrived, marveled at her skill but felt compelled to question her. "Madam," he said, "you seem to combine in yourself a sick-diet kitchen and a medical staff. May I inquire under whose authority you are working?"

Without pausing in her work, she answered him, "I have received my authority from the Lord God Almighty; have you anything that ranks higher than that?"

The truth of the matter was that she was under nobody's authority but her own. Eventually, she received government permission to serve the troops, but it was a mere formality. She had always taken matters into her own hands and always would.

> She was loved by the patients, trusted by the generals, feared and respected by those in between.

Getting Supplies

One time Bickerdyke finagled some bath water. Cleanliness was next to godliness; it also saved lives. After the battle at Corinth, Mississippi, the well at Academy Hospital ran dry. When General Stephen Augustus Hurlbut was brought in on a stretcher with a severe chill, Mother Bickerdyke insisted that several men carry water from a spring, in barrels, and heat it on the kitchen stove.

After the general had a good soak, that very same water bathed 16 men right off the battlefield. They needed it a lot more than the general, but it would never have been hauled and heated just to wash soldiers.

Supplying the hospitals with food was serious business, but once Mother B. had a bit of fun with it. She applied for 30 days' leave to go to the North and fetch fresh eggs and milk. A doctor in Memphis said he knew she was pigheaded, but he hadn't thought she was daft! Didn't she know they'd spoil? No, she didn't think so. She'd just go get her leave approved by Hurlbut.

Back she came a month later, with 100 cows and 1,000 hens. Spoil indeed! She had put that doctor in his place!

Soldiers Came First

Generals knew not to underestimate Mary Ann Bickerdyke. Grant himself gave her a pass through the lines. General William Tecumseh

After a battle, Mother Bickerdyke would search long into the night for wounded soldiers in need of help.

Sherman trusted her with his military plans for the Georgia Campaign so that she would know where to expect casualties. Finally, on the morning of May 24, 1865, in Washington, D.C., the boom of a cannon signaled not battle, but the start of a parade. The war was over! At General John Logan's personal request, Bickerdyke rode next to him at the head of the 15th Corps.

Her boys had spent the night grooming her horse, Whitey, and covering his blanket with forget-me-nots. On his back, they had placed a brand new lady's sidesaddle. She had long wanted one, considering "riding astraddle" on an army saddle neither seemly nor comfortable. In her excitement over the gift, she had no time to change into the fine riding skirt given her by friends in New York. Instead, she took her place next to Logan in her everyday calico dress and sunbonnet. They nodded to Grant and Sherman in the reviewing stand and Logan said, "Come on, Mother. They're expecting us."

"Me? Land sakes, General, they don't want me up there."

"Yes, they do. General Sherman told me to be sure and bring you."

"Well, that's real nice of them, I must say. But I can't do it. You get along up there. I got work to do."

All day, the parade surged on. In Bickerdyke's first-aid tent, she refreshed her boys with lemonade and sandwiches. She applied cracked ice for sunstroke and dressings for blistered feet. The casualties were minor, and the occasion joyous. She could have been reviewing the parade in style, but, as always, her soldiers came first.

Key Players

Mary Ann Ball "Mother" Bickerdyke
(1817–1901)

During the Civil War, Mother Bickerdyke worked tirelessly to improve hospital conditions in Cairo, Illinois, and elsewhere. In 1861, Cairo was a busy city on the Ohio River where Union soldiers were stationed on their way to and from the front lines of the war. As her reputation for hard work and prompt action spread, Bickerdyke was asked to supervise the construction of about 300 field hospitals. After the Civil War, Bickerdyke continued to work in behalf of veterans.

Today, a statue of Bickerdyke kneeling before a wounded soldier stands in the city square of her hometown, Galesburg, Illinois.

Thaddeus Lowe's experiments with hot air balloons caught the attention of military leaders, who used them to keep an eye on enemy movements. Here a balloon is being inflated with hydrogen gas.

First Prisoner of the Civil War

The first prisoner of the Civil War was, surprisingly, not a general or a drummer boy. He was not even a soldier. He was a balloonist named Thaddeus Lowe. Lowe's strange adventure began in Cincinnati, Ohio. There, on April 19, 1861, he was preparing to make a balloon flight to the

East Coast. He had built his own balloon, which he called the *Enterprise*, for this flight.

Lowe had a dream. He wanted to be the first person to fly across the Atlantic Ocean in a balloon. But he knew he had to make a trial overland run first to test wind currents. That was why he was in Cincinnati.

The people of Cincinnati welcomed Lowe and held a banquet in his honor. It was an exciting occasion, and there was much discussion not only about Lowe and his flight, but also about the growing problems between the North and the South. Why, just last week the Confederates had fired on the Union post at Fort Sumter in South Carolina! Surely that meant war! It would be interesting to see how the new president, Mr. Abraham Lincoln, would handle this!

The Time Was Right

Late that evening, while the banquet was still going on, Lowe was told that the winds were right and the weather was perfect for a balloon ascension. When he heard this news, Lowe decided to leave immediately. He ordered the balloon to be filled and began last-minute preparations.

At three o'clock on the morning of April 20, Lowe stepped into the basket underneath the huge balloon and gave the signal to cast off. The *Enterprise* rose quickly into the sky. Lowe was on his way to the East Coast!

As the balloon sailed over the dark land, Lowe took instrument

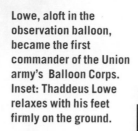

Lowe, aloft in the observation balloon, became the first commander of the Union army's Balloon Corps. Inset: Thaddeus Lowe relaxes with his feet firmly on the ground.

readings and made notes. The balloon rose to 5,000, then 10,000, then 15,000 feet. He was almost three miles above the earth! He

made some calculations and figured that he was traveling close to 100 miles per hour. He had never traveled that fast in a balloon before!

Drifting Off Course

On the horizon, Lowe saw the sky growing light. Morning was coming. Far in the distance Lowe could see the Blue Ridge Mountains. As his balloon drifted toward them, he realized that he was traveling more toward the southeast than true east. He recalled the talk he had heard about the war, and hoped he would have no problems when he landed.

The *Enterprise* climbed gracefully over the mountains. On the other side, Lowe passed over hills and farms and fields for several hours. Then, in the distance, he saw his goal. It was a great body of water — the Atlantic Ocean!

Lowe was tempted to go on, to try to cross the Atlantic, but he knew he was not prepared for such a flight. He would have to end his journey here. He opened a valve to lower the altitude of his balloon, and caught a wind current that carried him back inland.

Behind Enemy Lines

Lowe looked for a place to set the balloon down, but most of the land below him was too marshy. Finally, he spotted a ridge up ahead. It seemed a good place to land, so he dropped his balloon toward the earth.

Even before he landed, a small crowd gathered. Many of the men carried guns. As Lowe landed, no one in the crowd made any effort to help him.

"Hello!" Lowe called loudly. "Could one of you assist me in tying the balloon down?"

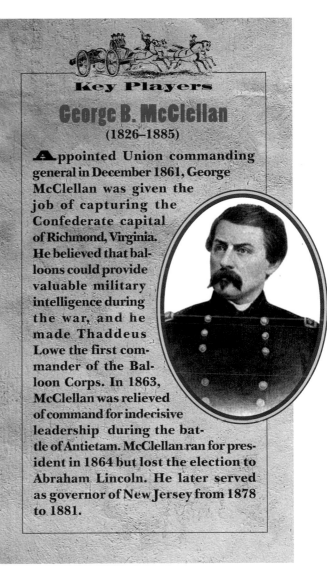

Key Players
George B. McClellan
(1826–1885)

Appointed Union commanding general in December 1861, George McClellan was given the job of capturing the Confederate capital of Richmond, Virginia. He believed that balloons could provide valuable military intelligence during the war, and he made Thaddeus Lowe the first commander of the Balloon Corps. In 1863, McClellan was relieved of command for indecisive leadership during the battle of Antietam. McClellan ran for president in 1864 but lost the election to Abraham Lincoln. He later served as governor of New Jersey from 1878 to 1881.

At first, no one moved. Then a tall woman grabbed one of the ropes and steadied the balloon as Lowe secured the other lines.

The people in the crowd did not know what to think of this man who had dropped out of the sky. None of them had ever seen a balloon before. "He's the devil," one man muttered, and others agreed.

Lowe realized he had better talk fast to save himself. "Allow me to introduce myself," he said. "I am Professor Thaddeus S.C. Lowe, balloonist, scientist, and inventor. I have just completed a journey from Cincinnati, Ohio, in this balloon."

Someone in the crowd said, "You hear that? He's a Northerner!"
"He's a spy!" someone else said. "He's a Yankee spy!"
"We should shoot him right here on this spot," said another planter.

Taken Prisoner

Suddenly the tall woman who had helped Lowe tie up the balloon spoke. "Hush up, all of you!" she said. "We'll do what is right. We'll take Professor Lowe to the county seat at Unionville. Someone get a wagon for his gear."

As a wagon was brought over, Lowe asked, "By the way, what state am I in?"

The tall woman smiled: "This place is called Pea Ridge in South Carolina. And since you are a Northerner, you'd better consider yourself a prisoner of the Confederate States of America!"

All of Lowe's equipment, including the balloon and basket, was loaded into the wagon, and the long, rough trip to Unionville began. They arrived late in the evening. The planters decided to take Lowe to an inn for the night and guard him there.

Now Lowe might have been in very serious trouble, but luck was with him. The innkeeper had seen Lowe fly his balloons before and knew the young scientist. The next morning, after a long talk with the town leaders, Lowe was released and put on a train. A few days later, he was back in Cincinnati, Ohio.

From Scientist to Spy

Lowe went on to become involved with the Union army. He convinced President Lincoln to allow him to act as a spy, using his balloon to carry him above enemy territory. He used a telegraph to communicate with Union forces on the ground. The Confederates were never able to shoot him down. Lowe was the first person in history to use aeronautics (aircraft navigation) to determine the strength and position of enemy forces.

Lowe also helped establish the 1st U.S. Balloon Corps. He never did make his journey across the Atlantic Ocean, but he was the first prisoner and one of the forgotten heroes of the Civil War.

Fast Fact

A Confederate army balloon made of multicolored silk was nicknamed the "Silk Dress Balloon."

Eye of History
Mathew Brady, Civil War Photographer

Mathew Brady, a native of Warren County, New York, was only 16 when he moved to New York City with a friend. The year was 1839. Brady worked as a jeweler's helper during the day and studied the new art of daguerreotype photography at night. In 1844, Brady believed he knew enough to establish his own studio and gallery on one of New York's busiest streets. It wasn't long before he became known as "Brady of Broadway." Many rich and famous people — former president John Quincy Adams, writer Edgar Allan Poe, singer Jenny Lind — came to his studio to have their portraits made.

On the Battlefield

Just before the start of the Civil War, Brady opened a second studio in Washington, D.C. Even though he was busy photographing princes, presidents, and poets, he wanted to go to war when the Civil War started.

"I felt I had to go,"

Brady wore a white linen duster, an artist's straw hat, and sturdy military boots, called jackboots, that reached above his knees.

23

he told a friend later, "to preserve the moment of experience for the future."

Brady began to dog the steps of General Winfield Scott, head of the Army of the Potomac, to get permission to accompany him to face the Confederate army. When Brady learned that Scott was going to be replaced, he went to President Abraham Lincoln for the desired permission. Lincoln scrawled "Pass Brady" on a piece of paper for him, but told Brady he must stay out of the way of the troops and pay for his own equipment.

Capturing the Action

Brady immediately hired photographic teams to capture the action in different locations. Each of Brady's photographic teams included a driver, a wagon pulled by two horses, the photographer, the photographer's assistant, and the printer to make the photographs from the glass plates. Brady and his men faced danger daily in their marches, and more than once a photography team found itself caught between the two armies.

While Brady was not the first war photographer, he was the first to put teams of photographers into the field to photograph all aspects of the battle. Because the name "Brady" was stamped on most of the photographs, it is difficult to determine which ones he took and which ones his assistants took.

Images of War

Brady told his photographers, "The camera is the eye of history…. You must never make bad pictures." The photographs they took showed grim scenes of war. They captured the utter desolation and cruelty of the war for the first time. They showed the grotesquely sprawled bodies of men, horses, and dogs in death, roofless crumbled houses, barns and fences, the wounded, the wrecked wagons, and unmanned cannon. Because exposures took about 30 seconds each, there were no action photographs, and the photographers had to use heavy tripods to hold their cameras still during the exposure time. In all, Brady and his photographers took more than 3,500 pictures of the Civil War.

Brady's health and eyesight, which had always been poor, became worse after the Civil War. In addition, he was faced with many debts from outfitting the photography wagons. Although he had published two earlier photo books, he was unable to find a backer to publish his Civil War photographs during his lifetime. In 1871, he went bankrupt. He died in 1896 and was buried in Arlington National Cemetery.

Key Players

Winfield Scott
(1786–1866)

Winfield Scott was commanding general of the Union army at the start of the Civil War. He was 75 years old at the time, and a veteran of both the War of 1812 and the U.S.–Mexican War. Scott died at West Point, New York, on May 29, 1866.

Preserving His Legacy

After his death, people who wanted to collect on Brady's outstanding debts seized many of the famous plates in lieu of payment. Some of the plates were broken and chipped while improperly stored in various government warehouses. Some were found in a barn in upstate New York. Others were lost forever.

"I felt I had to go [to war] to preserve the moment of experience for the future."

— **Mathew Brady**

Brady's heirs sold a large collection for $5,000 to the Library of

Congress in 1954. The library went on to acquire all the other known plates. They were catalogued, and in 1964 were finally opened for use by the public as Brady had wished.

Brady set out to "preserve the moment of experience," and his Civil War photographs are a treasured record of a dramatic chapter in American history.

'What-Is-It?'

Brady moved his bulky photographic equipment in an odd-looking, hearselike wagon, which onlookers began calling a "What-is-it?" because they had never seen anything like it before.

By today's standards, the cameras Brady used were huge and heavy. Instead of film, glass plates were used. Since no enlarging to speak of was done at that time, the cameras' plates were the same size as the photographs. Most of these plates were 8 by 10 inches in size, but some were as big as 12 by 16 inches.

Each team's equipment was extensive. There were glass plates, bottles containing the various chemical solutions, dishes in which to mix the solutions and develop the plates and photographs, measuring cups for the solutions, funnels, and a pail for rinse water. Some of the teams even carried barrels with their own water supplies.

By the end of the Civil War, Brady had 22 of his "What-is-it?" wagons assigned to many of the battlefields, including Antietam, Fredericksburg, Gettysburg, and Manassas.

Wild Rose and Aunt Sally

In her elegant home in Washington, D.C., Rose Greenhow, Confederate spy, was entertaining a Yankee captain. Outside, concealed in the shrubbery, was detective Allan Pinkerton on assignment to get the goods on "Wild Rose," the South's most effective spy. He boosted himself up on another detective's shoulders and peered into the window. He saw just what he had expected.

The blue-uniformed captain was pointing to a map. "DuPont will be moving south from Fortress Monroe with 77 vessels. He will depart on October 14th."

"This is very important information," said Rose. "I am grateful to you." The beautiful young widow smiled up at him.

"You owe me no thanks, Mrs. Greenhow," said the captain. "I am happy to serve just for the pleasure of your company."

Detective Pinkerton stepped down from his friend's shoulders. He had the evidence. He had seen Mrs. Greenhow accept a map from a Yankee. Tomorrow, he thought, I will put a man on her trail, and perhaps catch more of her spy ring.

Shopping for Secrets

The next day Rose made her daily shopping trip up and down the thin cobblestones of Pennsylvania Avenue. She was a pretty

Rose Greenhow, shown here with her daughter, was one of the South's best spies. Confederate president Jefferson Davis considered her assistance critical to the South's win at First Manassas in July 1861.

Abraham Lincoln (center) chose detective Allan Pinkerton (left) to head up the country's first Secret Service agency, to investigate plots and protect the president. In this photo, Pinkerton and Lincoln visit Antietam Battlefield in September 1862 to consult with General John A. McClernand (right).

picture as she smiled and waved at shopkeepers and passersby. A small plumed velvet hat sat on her shiny black hair. Her full black skirt nodded gracefully as she walked. A ruffle-topped parasol was swinging from her wrist.

At a sidewalk table, Rose picked out half a dozen large red apples, chatting all the while to the vendor.

"What do you hear from Aunt Sally?" she asked. "Aunt Sally" was a code name for the Confederacy.

"Nothing today, ma'am." The vendor put the apples into her string bag. He turned to the next customer.

"May I help you, sir?"

"Uh, no thanks." The man turned away from the table.

As she started on her way, Rose caught a glimpse of that man. "There's something familiar about him," she thought. "I have seen that curly brown hair and short beard before."

Followed

As she was entering a grocery shop, she stopped suddenly. As she expected, the man behind her was so close that he bumped right into her. And, as she expected, he had curly brown hair and a short beard. She continued into the shop and asked for some flour. The grocer talked as he scooped flour from a barrel.

"You'll be glad to hear that Aunt Sally has better use of her legs. The medicine you suggested was just the right thing." "Legs" was the code word for infantry. "Medicine" was the word for maps.

He handed the sack of flour to Rose and turned to the man who had bumped into her.

"May I help you, sir?"

"Yes, I, uh, need some sugar."

Rose smiled. "Remember me to Aunt Sally," she said as she left the shop.

A tall, thin man stepped out of a cobbler's shop as Rose passed. He bowed and took her elbow. They walked along together slowly.

"Such a wonderful dinner party at your home last week, Mrs. Greenhow. I have not forgotten our talk there. And I have seen your Aunt Sally since then."

"That's very good of you to keep in touch with her," answered Rose. "I fear, though, that it is getting late. I wonder if you could tell me the correct time."

Passing Notes

The man slowed his step as he took a gold watch from his vest pocket and looked at it. Then he put the watch back into the pocket, and he pulled two envelopes from an inside coat pocket. Rose took these from him and slid them into her skirt pocket in one swift motion.

"It's just 12:00, Mrs. Greenhow."

"Oh dear, I must go now."

"There was one more thing I wanted to tell you about Aunt Sally...."

Battle of the Spies

Spies were everywhere during the Civil War. They were passionate about their work and determined to win the war for their side at any cost. It was not difficult for a Northerner to pass himself (or herself) off as a Southerner, and vice versa. And there was little if any law enforcement to stop the flow of information. Even newspaper reporters picked up on secret military plans and reported troop movements before they happened!

Suddenly Rose dropped her purse. The young man stooped to pick it up. He handed it to her.

"Thank you," said Rose as she took it. "Oh my, this silly old clasp has opened now, and I can't close it again." Her fingers fumbled, and the man bent to help her.

A folded paper dropped from the man's hand into the purse.

"Thank you again," said Rose.

She walked on alone, nodding at neighbors who sat at their windows on this hot day.

As she approached her house, a man on the corner began to whistle. This was a signal to her that there was trouble ahead.

Tilting her parasol to hide her face from the street as she passed, she whispered to the man, "If I touch my hat, warn the others away."

A few steps later, she stopped a moment to take a handkerchief from her purse. As her fingers grasped the soft material, they also grasped the folded note. The detective saw her pat her perspiring face with the handkerchief, but he did not see her slip the note into her mouth. Holding back the urge to gag, she pressed the note with her tongue until it was soft enough to swallow.

"There are some men in your house," called a neighbor from a window. "They went in without knocking. I think they are looking for Aunt Sally."

So she was caught!

Surrounded

Detective Pinkerton stood between her and her front door.

"Mrs. Greenhow, I place you under arrest."

"Sir, you have no right to be on my property."

"I charge you with treason. Now we will search your house. Stand out of the way."

"Yankee manners! No Confederate would talk to a woman in such a way! If I were a man, sir, you would not dare...."

Then the other detective was on the front steps, too. Two more were running down the street toward them. Rose lifted her hand to her hat. She held it there a moment, almost like a salute. This would warn the others not to walk into a trap.

The men surrounded Rose, and they entered the house together. Rose's anger turned to fear as she began to think of all the material they would find. Suddenly, she thought of the most valuable piece of evidence in the house. It was the key to the code. It was in a briefcase hidden on the very top of the library bookshelves.

The Search

As she watched, the men pulled clothing from closets, over-turned desk drawers, inspected wastebaskets, even ripped trimmings from dresses and hats. They found maps under couches, notes in vases, coded messages in bureau drawers.

In her library, they found packets and packets of letters. "Mail from William Seward, James Buchanan, Martin Van Buren! All the important men of the country have written to you!" exclaimed Pinkerton.

Rose said nothing. The only letters she could save now were the ones in her skirt pocket. Then she had an idea.

"Sir, I am going to retire to my room. I find myself exhausted from watching this destruction of my property."

"Very well, ma'am. But we will be watching you."

Rose stared daggers at him and then swept out the door in a swish of taffeta.

She went into the bedroom and shut the door. She looked under the bed, behind the drapes, in the closet. No detectives! "I must get that briefcase from the library," she thought, "and I must get rid of the letters in my pocket."

Sitting on the bed, she tore the letters into tiny pieces. Then she got down on her hands and knees and scattered the pieces under the carpet as far back as she could.

> "I must get that briefcase from the library," she thought, "and I must get rid of the letters in my pocket."

She had barely stood up again when a woman detective entered without knocking.

"I'll search you now," she said.

"I can't believe the horror of this whole experience," Rose sputtered and complained while she was being searched. But her thoughts were on the briefcase in the library.

"Please tell Detective Pinkerton that this is one more indignity he will have to pay for," said Rose to the woman as she was leaving. "And tell him that I demand he summon my friend Lily McCall to be with me. It is not proper that I be left alone with all these Yankee men."

Creating a Distraction

A few hours later, Lily arrived at Rose's door. After a quick embrace, the women got right to work.

"Lily, the key to the code is in the library. We must get it before they find it."

"I'll see what I can do."

Lily left. She returned about half an hour later.

"Rose, the man who is guarding your room is Captain Dennis, an old friend of mine. He will be very happy to have me show him where the rum is kept later tonight. After things are quiet around here, he and I will go down cellar." She smiled. "We will be very busy there. And you can go to the library and get the briefcase."

The moon had been up a while when Rose opened her door noiselessly. There was no guard outside her door. Muted sounds were coming from another part of the house.

Probably they're all down cellar drinking my rum, she thought.

Rose tried to think only of the code. She didn't want to think about the creak of the stairs, the rustle of her dress, the possibility of bumping into furniture as she made her way down the dark stairs and across the long hall.

What was that noise? Was it breathing? Her eyes found the sound, and saw a form slouched on a chair in the hall.

She glided in front of the sleeping guard and into the library.

Slowly and carefully, she moved to the bookshelves. Her skirt brushed against the stool, and she carried it over to the shelves. Then she climbed onto it. Her hands patted the top shelf. Then they touched leather. The case was open. The papers were there. She almost sighed in relief.

Down from the stool. Across the room. Past the guard. Up the stairs.

Protecting the Code

She had just shut her door and collapsed on the bed when the door opened again.

It was Lily. "Rose, did you get them?"

"Yes, Lily, and you must take them out with you. We'll tear them up, and you can put the pieces in your shoes."

Captain Dennis had enjoyed the rum, and his head hurt when he awoke the next morning. He was glad to let Lily go home. One less spy to watch, he thought.

From the bedroom window, Rose watched Lily go down the street. "A good day's work," she thought. "The code is safe."

Rose Greenhow continued to spy for the Confederates even while under house arrest. The Yankees moved her to a small, dirty, windowless cell in the Old Capitol Prison. Still she kept up her spying. When the Yankees found they were unable to stop her, they finally let her free on the condition that she never return to Northern territory.

Fast Fact

Confederate spy Rose Greenhow lived just

2 blocks

from the White House.

When General Grant Lost His Cool

General Ulysses S. Grant was known for his quiet, reflective personality when he commanded Union forces during the Civil War. His calm composure, even under the most trying of battlefield conditions, was a source of wonderment to his associates, as was his aversion to the use of profanity and to the inhumane treatment of animals — two frailties that were all too common among fighting soldiers.

The nearest Grant came to losing his temper in the presence of his close associate and aide, Colonel Horace Porter, was once during an especially critical engagement late in the war, when the general's party happened upon the scene of a Union teamster utterly beside himself with fury, trying in vain to persuade a team of horses to pull an army wagon out of a mud hole.

The agitated teamster was whipping and flogging the horses and reviling them in the most abusive terms when Grant rode up. Leaping from his saddle and clenching his fists as he ran, Grant charged up to the offending soldier and demanded, "What does this conduct mean? Stop beating those horses!"

The enraged teamster finally calmed down when he saw that the general meant business, but not before taking another healthy swing at the reluctant horses.

Grant ordered the man seized and disciplined on the spot. But the incident continued to rankle the mind of the commander, who mentioned it several times to Porter, even as bullets were flying around them in the heated battle that followed.

By nightfall, Grant was still upset and, over supper, was moved to say, "If people only knew how much more they could get out of a horse by gentleness than harshness, they would save a great deal of trouble for both the horse and the man.

"A horse is a particularly intelligent animal; he can be made to do almost anything if his master has the intelligence to let him know what is required...."

His confrontation with the teamster, wrote Porter in his memoirs, "was the one exhibition of temper manifested by Grant during the entire campaign, and the only one I ever witnessed during my many years of service with him," which included the postwar period when Grant was president.

Later, while sitting quietly around the campfire one night, Porter asked the leader of Union armies how it happened that

Throughout his life, Ulysses S. Grant had a special connection with horses. Among the many horses Grant owned, the three that were most dear to him were Egypt, Jeff Davis, and Cincinnati.

through all the rough-and-tumble of army service and frontier life, he had never been provoked into swearing. Grant replied thoughtfully, "Well, somehow or other, I never learned to swear. When a boy, I seemed to have an aversion to it, and when I became a man I saw the folly of it. I have always noticed, too, that swearing helps to rouse a man's anger. And when a man flies into a passion, his adversary who keeps cool always gets the better of him.

"In fact, I could never see the use of swearing. I think it is the case with many people who swear excessively that it is a mere habit, and that they do not mean to be profane. But, to say the least, it is a great waste of time."

Horse Sense

As a boy, Ulysses S. Grant loved horses and was very good at handling them. When he was just 10 years old, people who lived near the Grant family in Georgetown, Ohio, would bring their horses to Ulysses for training. By the time he was 12, Ulysses was an expert rider.

Everywhere they marched, the 8th Regiment of the Wisconsin Volunteers carried Old Abe with them. The eagle would often soar above the regiment, jabbering raucously, as if urging the men into action.

The Eagle That Went to War

I't's not every eagle that marches off to war. And gets wounded twice in battle, is decorated for bravery, and becomes a national hero. But then Old Abe wasn't just any kind of eagle....

The eaglet was just a fledgling, barely able to fly, nesting in an emerald pine tree in northwest Wisconsin one mild spring morning in 1861. From his perch atop Flambeau Hill, he could look out over

the rolling farm country. An occasional rifle shot he heard was from a hunter, not Civil War gunfire.

Taken From His Nest

Walking through the woods that morning came Chief Sky, an Indian of the Lac du Flambeau band of Chippewa. Looking up, he noticed the eaglet. Even a chief seldom took a chance raiding an eagle's nest. But since there was just one fledgling and no full-grown birds in sight, he climbed the tree.

The eaglet nipped his finger, but the chief managed to slip a small sack over the bird's head. Taking his prize, he climbed down from the tree, ran to his canoe, and paddled swiftly off up the Chippewa River.

Two days later, Chief Sky came to a farm owned by Daniel McCann, hoping to sell him the eaglet. The farmer was out working in his field, but his wife thought she'd like to keep the bird as a pet. She traded the chief a bag of corn and took the eaglet.

A 1904 Memorial Day poster features Old Abe nearly 50 years after the Civil War ended. To this day, the famous war eagle remains a Wisconsin hero and symbol of patriotism.

MAY 30. 1904

MEMORIAL DAY IN WISCONSIN SCHOOLS

When McCann came home and saw the eaglet, he said the bird would have to go. It would be too much trouble to keep. The next day, he took the bird to the town of Eau Claire and showed him to some young Wisconsin recruits on their way to Camp Randall at Madison. One of them, a young man named Johnny Hill, took a special liking to the bird.

Old Abe Joins the Army

"We need a mascot in this war we're going to," Hill told his comrades. "Let's buy him and take him along with us."

"How much?" the other recruits asked.

Mr. McCann decided that he wanted to be rid of the eaglet more than he wanted to make a lot of money, especially off of recruits going to war.

"Two dollars and a half?" he asked.

Hill and his companions dug into their pockets and among them came up with the money. The sale was made, and the eaglet now found himself going off to war. Hill christened him Old Abe, after President Abraham Lincoln, and they took the eaglet in as a full-fledged recruit in the Union army.

A few days later, they marched into Camp Randall with Old Abe. They were a little afraid they might get their mascot killed and themselves court-martialed for bringing a wild eagle into the army.

But the commander, knowing the importance of morale to a unit, thought an eagle for a mascot was a fine idea. A perch was made for Old Abe in the form of a shield on which the Stars and Stripes were painted along with the inscription "Eighth Regiment, Wisconsin Volunteers."

Place of Honor

This illustration comes from an article about Old Abe that appeared in the October 14, 1861, edition of the *New York Illustrated News.*

The metal perch was mounted on a five-foot pole. A bearer, by setting the staff in a belt-socket, held Old Abe up at a station assigned him at the center of the line of march, behind the Union flag.

A short time later, the commander nicknamed the regiment "the Eagles," and Old Abe was formally sworn into the U.S. Army and bedecked in red, white, and blue ribbons.

His fame already had begun to spread, and a businessman in St. Louis offered to buy Old Abe for $500, but he wasn't for sale.

Old Abe went with the Wisconsin Eagles on their mission to war. After he overcame his initial surprise at the sound of enemy gunfire, he would scream fiercely, especially when the company advanced.

Civil War Mascots

During the Civil War, many army regiments had animal mascots. These animals were faithful friends to the men. They shared the life of a soldier in the camp and on the battlefield. Many regiments had dogs. Several had badgers. Others had squirrels. And one even carried a mouse in a cigar box. All these animals loved the soldiers and reminded them of home.

Dick (sheep, 2nd Rhode Island Infantry) amused the men by marching with the officers on dress parade.

Several regiments had **bears** that went into battle. One weighed 300 pounds.

Jack (terrier, 102nd Pennsylvania Infantry) The men of Jack's regiment bought him a silver collar that said: "Jack: the hero of many battles."

Susan Jane (pig, Stonewall Brigade) was bought to be eaten, but the soldiers loved her so much that they kept her as a mascot.

The men of the 11th Pennsylvania Volunteer Infantry loved **Sallie Ann Jarrett** (Staffordshire bull terrier) so much that they placed a statue of her at Gettysburg National Military Park.

Jake (gamecock, 3rd Tennessee Regiment) was captured with his regiment and was sent to prison with them. He lived to be sent home with his regiment.

Douglas (camel, 43rd Missippi Company A) carried officers' baggage and was very friendly with the horses.

He would jabber raucously and often soar overhead as if scouting, then return to his perch and call noisily, as if urging the men to action.

Symbol of Courage

Everywhere it marched, the regiment became famous, not only because of its mascot, but because of its bravery. Old Abe was always there, in the thick of 36 battles and skirmishes, a symbol of courage to Johnny Hill and every other soldier.

One Confederate general remarked that he would rather capture "that sky buzzard" than a whole brigade of soldiers.

Old Abe suffered two minor battle wounds, at Corinth and Vicksburg, Mississippi, before the war ended. When the Wisconsin Eagles returned to Madison, the soldiers marched through the streets carrying Old Abe bobbing on his perch, hale and hearty as ever. Crowds cheered him as a real hero, and he flapped his wings as a sign of recognition.

In Retirement

With the war over, Old Abe was presented to the state of Wisconsin and given a room in the basement of the capitol, where a soldier comrade became his private caretaker. Hill, who also had survived the war, visited him often.

The Civil War's most famous eagle, perched on a cannon, strikes a stunning pose. Old Abe lived nearly 20 years, basking in the celebrity of a state and national hero.

Thousands of people from all over the country came to see the famous war eagle that had survived so many battles and spurred so many soldiers on to victory. His moulted feathers sold for $5 apiece, and the famous circus owner P.T. Barnum offered $20,000 to feature him as a circus performer. But other work was in store for Old Abe.

By special act of the Wisconsin legislature in 1876, and with the governor's approval, Old Abe was exhibited at the U.S. Centennial Exposition in Philadelphia. His chaperone was none other than his old army buddy, Johnny Hill.

Returning from Philadelphia, Old Abe went on tours of the country. He helped raise thousands of dollars for war relief charity and became a national hero all over again.

Old Abe was almost 20 years old when he died. A granite statue of the valiant eagle stands over the arched entrance to Old Camp Randall in Madison.

The Yankees Are Coming!

Many stories of the Civil War were never published in books or newspapers. They were told to family members who passed the stories down through the generations. This is one such story. It tells of a young girl's frightening experience when she came face to face with the enemy at her home near Savannah, Georgia.

Union general William Tecumseh Sherman captured Atlanta, Georgia, in September 1864 after four months of relentless battle. In November, he led his troops on a destructive path through the state to the port city of Savannah. This became known as Sherman's March to the Sea. The Union troops far outnumbered the Confederate soldiers stationed along the way, and the Southern troops were forced to surrender Savannah on December 21.

Here is one girl's story.

I was just a little girl — a very little girl — but old enough to know that something terrible was happening. Mother and Dad lived out from Savannah on a large farm. Dad grew everything we needed as well as cotton and tobacco. We had cows, horses, pigs, chickens — I guess about everything one could have living in the country.

I shall always remember a particular day in 1864. One of our neighbors came riding up to the house digging the spurs into the horse's sides. He arrived in a cloud of dust with his horse frothing at the mouth. My father was not home at the time, but my mother came running out. The boy was waving his arms and yelling at the top of his voice, "The Yankees are coming! General Sherman has burned up Atlanta and is on his way to Savannah. He is destroying everything in his path. Save what you can! He'll be here soon. I've got to warn the others."

My sister Idel had a high fever and was upstairs in her bed. Mother told everyone to take the silver and hide it under Idel's bed. She told our Mammy to sit on a sack of potatoes and spread her wide apron over it. She told Mammy's little boy to take a cow and run across the creek to a spot where he would be completely hidden.

Mother had only a short time to make those decisions, because soon there was a loud commotion as horses and soldiers filled up the yard. I was frightened and hid behind mother's skirt.

There was an exchange of words between the soldier in command and Mother. She told him she had a daughter quite ill upstairs who should

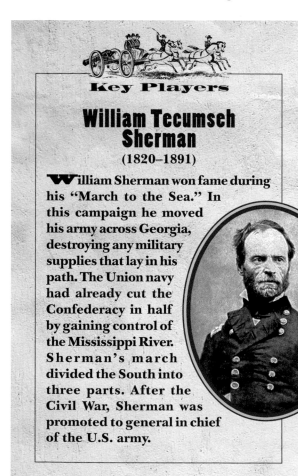

Key Players

William Tecumsch Sherman

(1820–1891)

William Sherman won fame during his "March to the Sea." In this campaign he moved his army across Georgia, destroying any military supplies that lay in his path. The Union navy had already cut the Confederacy in half by gaining control of the Mississippi River. Sherman's march divided the South into three parts. After the Civil War, Sherman was promoted to general in chief of the U.S. army.

On farms from Atlanta to Savannah, Union soldiers confiscated or destroyed crops and livestock to impoverish the South and starve the Confederacy.

not be disturbed, and so a soldier was placed in front of her door to keep the others from entering her room. But everything of any value was taken from the rest of the house. Some of the soldiers set fire to the grain fields, while others killed the hogs and chickens. They took everything they could and destroyed whatever they couldn't take. I remember my sister Inez had a pet horse who was old, lame, and blind in one eye. When Inez saw one of the soldiers leading her horse away, she ran after him crying and screaming, kicking and biting, until he finally left the horse with her.

After the soldiers finally left, the heads of the hogs were gathered and the meat was scraped off and cooked. We ate a lot of burnt corn. I guess we were fortunate that our house wasn't burned to the ground. Many were.

By the time Sherman's army reached Savannah, the path they had made through Georgia was 60 miles wide and 300 miles long. The Union soldiers were ordered to destroy the factories, farms, and railroads in order to cripple the Confederacy. Sherman's march proved a decisive blow, ensuring the South's defeat.

CIVIL WAR

1860

NOV 6
Abraham Lincoln is elected 16th president of the United States.

Lincoln

1861

FEB 9
Formation of the Confederate States of America (CSA) by secessionist states South Carolina, Mississippi, Florida, Alabama, Georgia, Louisiana, and Texas. Jefferson Davis elected CSA president.

Davis

MAR 4
Lincoln's inauguration

APR 12

Fort Sumter (South Carolina) Civil War begins with Confederate attack under Gen. Pierre Beauregard.

APR 15
Lincoln issues proclamation calling

for 75,000 troops. Gen. Winfield Scott becomes commander of Union army.

APR 17
Virginia joins CSA, followed by Arkansas, Tennessee, and North Carolina.

APR 20
Gen. Robert E. Lee resigns from U.S. Army and accepts command in Confederate army.

JUL 21
First Manassas (Virginia) Gen. Thomas J. "Stonewall" Jackson defeats Gen. Irvin McDowell.

NOV 1
Gen. George B. McClellan assumes command of Union forces.

1862

FEB 11-16
Fort Donelson (Tennessee) Gen. Ulysses S. Grant breaks major Confederate stronghold.

MAR
McClellan begins Peninsular Campaign, heading to Richmond,

Virginia, the Confederate capital.

APR 6-7
Shiloh (Tennessee) Grant defeats Beauregard and Gen. A.S. Johnston. Heavy losses on both sides.

APR 24

New Orleans (Louisiana) Gen. David Farragut leads 17 Union gunboats up Mississippi River and takes New Orleans, the South's most important seaport.

JUN 25-JUL 1
Seven Days (Virginia) Six major battles are fought over seven days near Richmond, Virginia. Lee is victorious, protecting the Confederate capital from Union occupation.

Halleck

JUL 18
Lincoln turns over command to Gen. Henry W. Halleck.

AUG 29-30
Second Manassas (Virginia) Jackson and Gen. James Longstreet defeat Gen. John Pope.

SEP 17
Antietam (Maryland) McClellan narrowly defeats Lee. Bloodiest day in American military history: 23,000 casualties.

SEP 22

Lincoln issues preliminary Emancipation Proclamation, freeing slaves in Confederate states.

OCT 3-4
Corinth (Mississippi) Gen. William Rosecrans defeats Gen. Earl Van Dorn.

44

NOTE: Battles are in black type, with flags indicating: Union victory ▄▄ Confederate victory ▄▄

TIME LINE

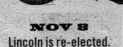

NOV 7
Lincoln replaces McClellan with Gen. Ambrose Burnside to lead Army of the Potomac.

Burnside

DEC 13
Fredericksburg (Virginia)
Lee defeats Burnside.

1863

JAN 1
Final Emancipation Proclamation frees slaves in Confederate states. Union army begins enlisting black soldiers.

JAN 25
Lincoln replaces Burnside with Gen. Joseph Hooker.

Hooker

JAN 29
Grant is placed in command of the Union army in the West.

MAY 1-4
Chancellorsville (Virginia)
Lee defeats Hooker.

JUN 28
Lincoln replaces Hooker with Gen. George E. Meade.

JUL 1-3

Gettysburg (Pennsylvania)
Meade defeats Lee.

JUL 4
Vicksburg (Mississippi)
After weeks of seige, Grant takes the Confederate stronghold on Mississippi River, effectively dividing eastern and western Confederate forces.

SEP 18-20
Chickamauga (Georgia)
Gen. Braxton Bragg defeats Rosecrans.

OCT 16
Lincoln puts Grant in charge of all western operations.

NOV 19
Lincoln delivers the Gettysburg Address, dedicating the battlefield as a national cemetery.

NOV 23-25
Chattanooga (Tennessee)
Grant defeats Bragg.

1864

MAR 9
Lincoln puts Grant in command of entire Union army. Gen. William T. Sherman takes over western operations.

MAY 8-21
Spotsylvania (Virginia)
Grant defeats Lee.

MAY 31-JUN 12
Cold Harbor (Virginia)
Lee defeats Grant and Meade.

JUN 15-18

Petersburg (Virginia)
Lee and Beauregard defeat Grant and Meade.

Lee

NOV 8
Lincoln is re-elected.

NOV 15-DEC 21

Sherman's "March to the Sea." Sherman destroys supplies and transportation systems from Atlanta to Savannah (Georgia), crippling the Confederacy.

1865

APR 2
Petersburg (Virginia)
Grant defeats Lee. Confederates leave Richmond.

APR 9
Lee surrenders to Grant at Appomattox Court House, Virginia.

APR 14
Lincoln is shot by John Wilkes Booth at Ford's Theatre, Washington, D.C. He dies the following morning.

DEC 6
Thirteenth Amendment to the Constitution abolishing slavery is ratified.

GRAPHICS BY FRED CARLSON

Glossary

Aeronautics: The design and construction of aircraft; also, aircraft navigation.

Assassinate: To murder an important person, usually for political reasons.

Brigade: A military combat unit commanded by a brigadier general or a colonel.

Campaign: In military terms, a series of battles, or other operations, in a particular area to accomplish a specific goal.

Casualties: In war, the victims: the injured, killed, captured, or missing in action.

Civil war: A war fought between people of the same nation.

Confederacy: In the American Civil War, the alliance of states that broke ties with the U.S. government to form a new government, called the Confederate States of America. The states that did not secede supported the Union.

Constitution: The basic set of laws that define a government and guide its decisions and direction.

Convalescent: A person who is gradually regaining strength after a sickness or injury.

Corps: In the military, a separate combat division with a special assignment.

Counterfeit: To make an imitation of something; often refers to fake money.

Court-martialed: When a member of the military is accused of a crime and tried by a military court.

Daguerreotype: One of the earliest methods of photography; a photograph made on a light-sensitive metal plate.

Dysentery: An intestinal ailment, usually caused by a parasite, causing severe abdominal pain, fever, and diarrhea.

Inauguration: The formal beginning of a term in office.

Mascot: An animal, usually, that is believed to bring good luck to the group, team, or unit it represents.

Morale: The attitude of a group or individual; a measure of cheerfulness, confidence, or willingness.

Pneumonia: A disease of the lungs that makes breathing very difficult.

Profanity: Vulgar language that is unacceptable in polite society.

Rebel: A person who opposes the authority in power. In the Civil War, "Rebel" became another word for Confederate. A *rebellion* occurs when a large group of rebels band together to fight the governing authority.

Recruit: noun — a new member of an organization, often the military; verb — to persuade someone to join an organization, often the military.

Regiment: A military unit of ground troops. *Regimental* refers to something orderly and strict.

Secede: To make a formal withdrawal from an organization, alliance, or, in American history, a nation. Secession occurred when 11 states officially withdrew from the United States of America and formed a new nation, the Confederate States of America.

Shoddy: Of poor quality; cheap, shabby.

Skirmish: A small conflict between enemies that may often lead to a larger battle.

Sovereignty: Independence and self-government.

Teamster: A person who drives a team of animals (more recently, a truck) carrying goods and supplies.

Treason: A deliberate action that betrays one's country, such as aiding its enemies.

Yankee: A person from the northeastern United States. During the Civil War, "Yankee" was another name for a Union soldier.

Index

COBBLESTONE®

The CIVIL WAR Series

Few events in our nation's history have been as dramatic as those leading up to and during the Civil War. People held strong views on each side of the Mason-Dixon line, and the clash of North and South had far-reaching consequences for our country that are still being felt today.

Each 48-page book delivers the solidly researched content COBBLESTONE® is known for, written in an engaging manner that is sure to retain the attention of young readers. Perfect for report research or pursuing an emerging interest in the Civil War, these resources will complete your collection of materials on this important topic.

Each sturdy, hardcover volume includes:
- Fair and balanced depictions of people and events
- Well-researched text ■ Historical photographs
- Glossary ■ Time line

$17.95 each

NATION AT WAR: SOLDIERS, SAINTS, AND SPIES	COB67900
YOUNG HEROES OF THE NORTH AND SOUTH	COB67901
ABRAHAM LINCOLN: DEFENDER OF THE UNION	COB67902
GETTYSBURG: BOLD BATTLE IN THE NORTH	COB67903
ANTIETAM: DAY OF COURAGE AND SACRIFICE	COB67904
ROBERT E. LEE: DUTY AND HONOR	COB67905
ULYSSES S. GRANT: CONFIDENT LEADER AND HERO	COB67906
STONEWALL JACKSON: SPIRIT OF THE SOUTH	COB67907
JEFFERSON DAVIS AND THE CONFEDERACY	COB67908
REBUILDING A NATION: PICKING UP THE PIECES	COB67909

Buy 3 books and get our Time Line Poster FREE!